I0223455

Copyright © 2022 by Myneesha King

All rights reserved under the Pan-American and International Copyright Conventions.

This book may not be reproduced, in whole or in part, in form or by any means electronic or mechanical, including photocopying, recording, or by any information storage and retrieval system now known or hereafter invented, without written permission from the publisher, The Kings' Press, LLC.

Published in the United States of America First published as
The Kings' Press, LLC paperback 2022

For information about permission to reproduce selections from this book, write to:

The Kings' Press, LLC
933 Louise Avenue Ste. 422 Charlotte,
North Carolina 28204

OR

Email:
thekingspressllc@gmail.com

Subjects: LCHS:

Family | K-12 Education | African American Authors | Children Books

Editing done by Ron King Jr., M.Ed.

For more information go to:
www.kingspresspublishing.com

Contact Email: thekingspressllc@gmail.com
ISBN: 978-1-7368791-0-8

About Author

Myneesha King

Born in the historic Homewood-Brushton community of Pittsburgh, Pennsylvania; Myneesha King is an alumnus of North Carolina Agricultural and Technical State University with a Bachelor of Fine Arts degree in Professional Theatre.

As a result of her dedication and attentiveness as a mother, she recounts memorable conversations had with her young son Josiah regarding angels. When Josiah was a toddler, he made a profound statement that sparked the concept for this book. Myneesha has fulfilled many roles as an actress, playwright, stage manager, director, and licensed educator in a variety of organizations, including The Hill House Association, The August Wilson Center for African American Culture, Pittsburgh Playwrights & Kuntu Repertory Theatres, Kingsley Association, Small Seeds Development Inc., Pittsburgh Public Schools, KIPP Charter School, Charlotte Mecklenburg Schools, Cabarrus County School and much more. Myneesha lives in Charlotte, North Carolina, with her husband and three children. She is co-founder of the publishing house, The Kings' Press LLC, where she is director of marketing and promotions.

An Aunt Like Mine

My aunt doesn't have children of her own. I'm most important to her. How do I know you ask? I'll tell you.

She says it to just about everyone she speaks to over the phone.

My aunt teaches me how to cook.

She makes sure
I'm learning and
reading good books.

She teaches me to eat healthy and how to dress.

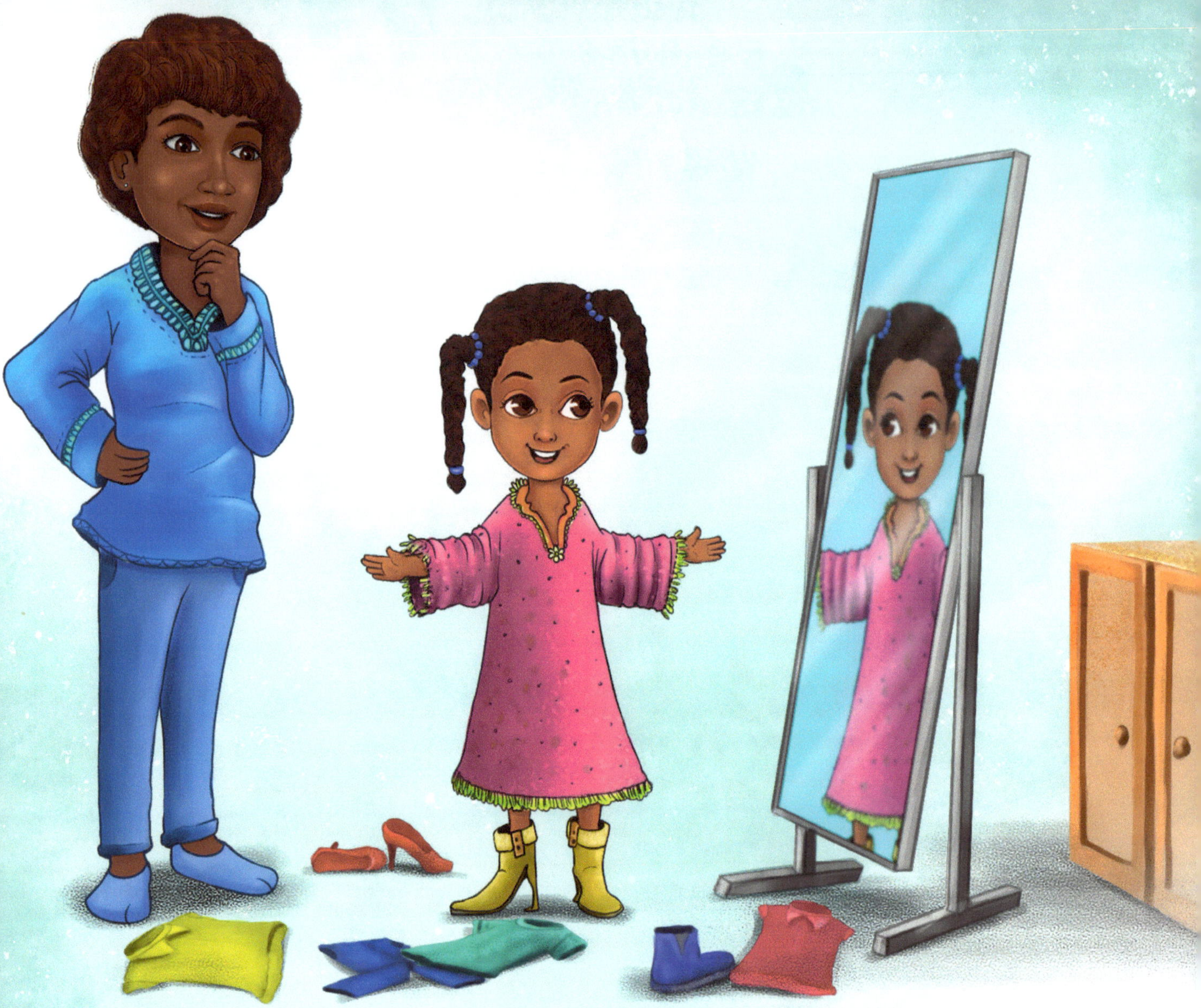

My aunt encourages me, pays attention to my needs

and challenges me to be my best.

She throws me great parties, not just for birthdays, but holidays too.

She makes sure I know what it means to be a good friend and stay honest in all that I do.

Her knack for **words**
makes **listening** to her
worth your while.

She'd say, "You have to live your life for you." Those words always were followed with a smile.

When **I'm with** my **aunt,**
I **don't have** a care in the world.

I know **I'm special** to **her.**
In fact, her **nickname** for me
is "**my favorite girl.**"

15

She loves to style my hair
and keeps me sitting pretty.

She's the best aunt
in the whole wide world,
especially to this kiddy!

There's nothing **my aunt** won't do for **me**

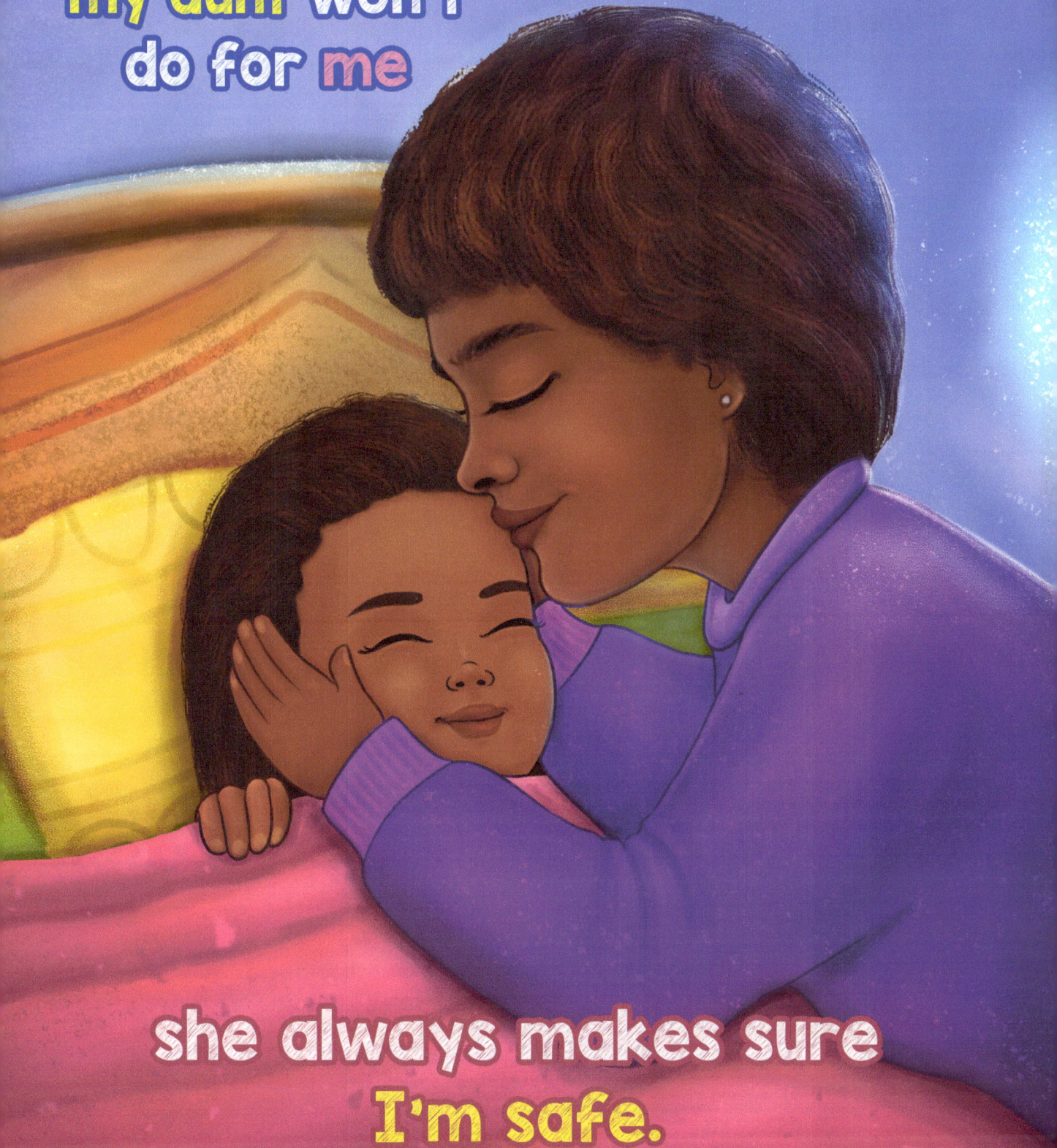

she always makes sure
I'm safe.

In moments when I'm bored, she becomes my best playmate.

She teaches me good lessons, wise sayings, and how to handle tough times.

I think it's only right that every kid in the world has an amazing aunt like mine.

DISCUSSION/QUIZ QUESTIONS

1. GIVE THREE EXAMPLES OF HOW THE GIRL'S AUNT MADE HER FEEL SPECIAL

2. WHAT ARE TWO ACTIVITIES THAT HER AUNT DID WITH HER?

3. DESCRIBE WHAT THE LITTLE GIRL IS DOING WHEN SHE SAYSHER AUNT MAKES HER FEEL "SAFE"

4. WHAT DOES HER AUNT TELL HER ABOUT LIFE?

5. HOW DOES THE LITTLE GIRL KNOW SHE IS "MOST IMPORTANT" TO HER AUNT?

King's Press Publishing

Real people. Powerful stories. Infinite Possibilities

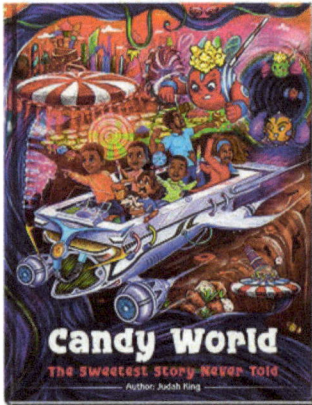

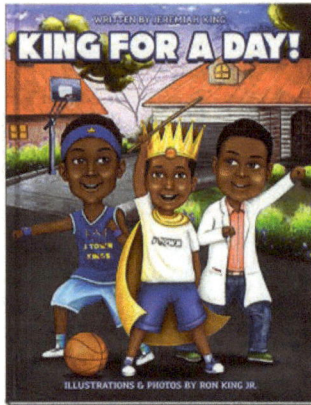

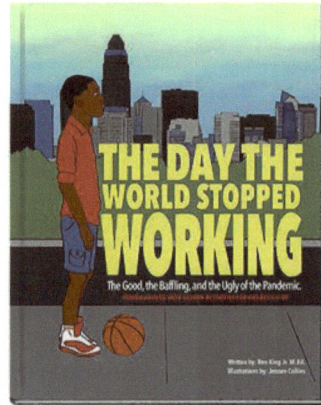

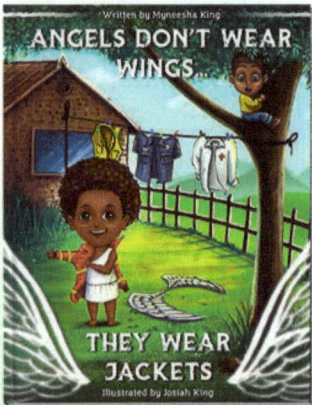

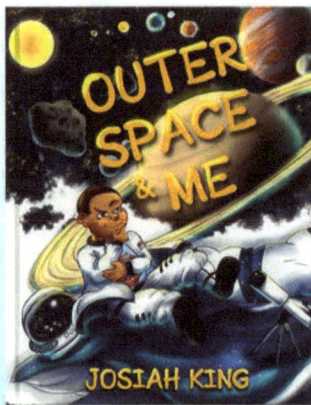

www.kingspresspublishing.com

www.ingramcontent.com/pod-product-compliance
Lightning Source LLC
Chambersburg PA
CBHW042012080426
42734CB00002B/59